The Library
of the
PILGRIMS

The Pilgrims Before the Mayflower

Susan Whitehurst

The Rosen Publishing Group's
PowerKids Press™
New York

To Whitney, for her courage

Published in 2002 by The Rosen Publishing Group, Inc.
29 East 21st Street, New York, NY 10010

First Edition

Book Design: Maria E. Melendez
Project Editor: Frances E. Ruffin

Photo Credits: Title page (pilgrims and holly tree) © SuperStock; title page (Scrooby vicarage), (Scrooby parish church) © Rose Beddinton; pp. 7, 11
© The Granger Collection; pp. 8, 9, 12, 14, 16, 17, 19 © North Wind Picture Archives; p. 22 © Mary Evans Picture Library; pp. 4, 6, 15, 20
© Bettmann/CORBIS; p. 18 (Pilgrim couple) © Lake County Museum/CORBIS.

Whitehurst, Susan.
The Pilgrims before the Mayflower / Susan Whitehurst.
     p. cm. — (The library of the Pilgrims)
Includes bibliographical references and index.
ISBN 0-8239-5811-6 (library binding)
1. Pilgrims (New Plymouth Colony)—Juvenile literature. 2. Separatists—England—History—17th century—Juvenile literature.
3. Separatists—Netherlands—Leiden—History—17th century—Juvenile literature. 4. Massachusetts—History—New Plymouth, 1620–1691—Juvenile
literature. 5. Leiden (Netherlands)—Church history—17th century—Juvenile literature. [1. Pilgrims (New Plymouth Colony) 2. Separatists.] I. Title.
F68 .W592 2002
974.4'8202—dc21

                                                                                                2001000250

Manufactured in the United States of America

Contents

How the Pilgrim Story Began

The story of the Pilgrims began long before they sailed to America on the *Mayflower* in 1620. Nearly 90 years earlier, King Henry VIII of England disagreed with the **Catholic** Pope. The Pope was the leader of all the **Christians** in Europe. The king formed a new church called the Church of England. He said everyone in England had to go to his church. This caused many problems. Not all of the people wanted to belong to his church. One group wanted to be separate from this church. They were called the **Separatists**. The Pilgrims came from this group.

This portrait shows King Henry VIII, of England, who made himself head of the Church of England.

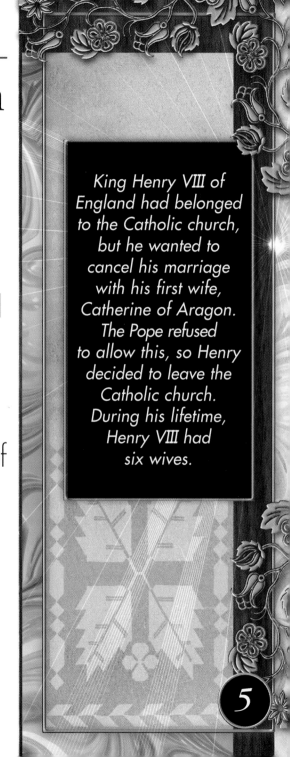

King Henry VIII of England had belonged to the Catholic church, but he wanted to cancel his marriage with his first wife, Catherine of Aragon. The Pope refused to allow this, so Henry decided to leave the Catholic church. During his lifetime, Henry VIII had six wives.

This engraving shows the Separatists at worship.

It took the Separatists several tries to leave England for Holland. They were arrested and put into jail many times before they were able to escape and reach Holland.

Separatists Jailed

In seventeenth-century England, it was a crime to belong to the Separatist Church. King James I could take away a Separatist's job, his house, or even throw him in jail. Forty Separatists met at William Brewster's home in Scrooby, England. They were called the Scrooby Separatists. Freedom of religion was so important to the Separatists that they met in spite of the risks. They learned that they could safely practice their religion in Holland. In 1607, the Scrooby Separatists sold their homes and walked over 50 miles (80 km) to meet a ship that would take them to Holland.

This is a photograph of Guildhall, an English prison where the Separatists were sent for trying to escape to Holland. The man shown is dressed in clothing of the 1600s.

Escape to Holland

The Dutch, who were the people of Holland, said they would welcome anyone of any faith who was well-behaved and honest. The Scrooby Separatists had learned that it was dangerous to leave England in large groups. They left in small groups and met in Amsterdam, Holland. An early group of Separatists spent about a year in Amsterdam waiting for other Separatists to join them. Then a group of 100 Separatists moved to the city of Leiden. They had no money and few belongings. Everything had been lost when they were arrested and jailed.

◀ *This hand-colored woodcut of a harbor in Amsterdam, Holland, is a scene of warehouses and ships being built.*

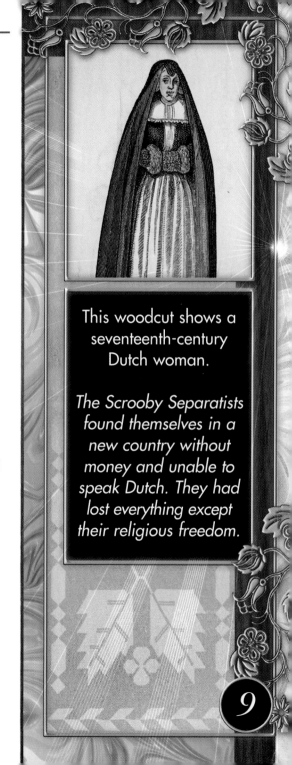

This woodcut shows a seventeenth-century Dutch woman.

The Scrooby Separatists found themselves in a new country without money and unable to speak Dutch. They had lost everything except their religious freedom.

9

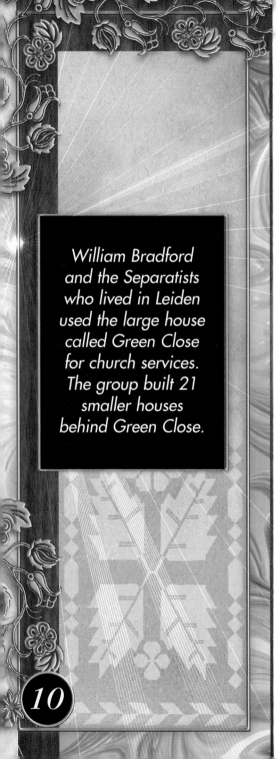

William Bradford and the Separatists who lived in Leiden used the large house called Green Close for church services. The group built 21 smaller houses behind Green Close.

Life in Leiden

Leiden was a beautiful city built on little islands joined by bridges. It was known as the city of **weavers**. In England the Separatists had been farmers. In Holland they became weavers, **merchants**, bakers, tailors, and carpenters. Many lived in poorhouses along dark, crowded alleys. In 1611, William Bradford, an English Separatist, **inherited** his father's land in England. He could not return to England because he'd be put in jail. Instead he had someone sell the land. Bradford and the group used the money to buy a large house in Leiden, called Green Close.

This is a portrait of William Bradford, who became a leader of the Separatists in Holland and later in America.

Time to Move Again

The Separatists, who later became the Pilgrims, might have stayed in Leiden and never have come to America. Several problems made them leave. An important fear was of the threat of war. Holland and Spain had had a great war before the Separatists moved to Holland. Both had agreed not to fight again for 12 years. Those 12 years were almost over. If Spain were to win a new war, Holland could lose its religious freedom. The Separatists did not want to suffer the same religious **persecution** they had suffered in England. It was time for them to move again.

The English Separatists were very concerned that their children were becoming more Dutch than English. Many of their children had been born in Holland, and they spoke Dutch. Some even joined the Dutch army.

◀ *This woodcut shows an English family in the 1600s.*

The English Separatists decided to move to North America. It promised to be a land of plenty. More important they would be free to practice their religion.

Where to Go?

The Separatists talked about leaving Holland in 1618. They knew they had to leave Holland, but they couldn't return to England. In England, Queen Elizabeth I and later King James I were the heads of the Church of England. They had had Separatists arrested, fined, whipped, and thrown in jail.

The Separatists thought about moving to South America, but the **climate** was so different from what they had experienced in Europe. North America was another possibility. They had heard that it was a place with fine land, **timber** for building houses, and a lot of fish, fruits, and birds.

Queen Elizabeth I was the daughter of Henry VIII and Anne Boleyn (1533–1603). She was cruel to the Separatists.

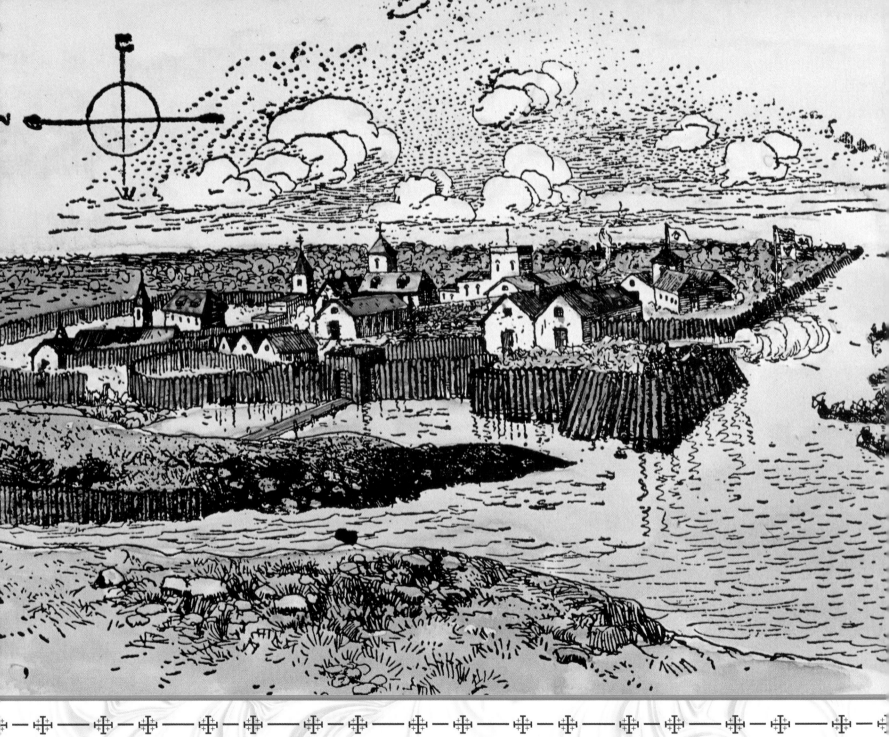

Three More Years

English people had already started a small **colony** in Virginia, called Jamestown. The Separatists had to ask King James if they could settle there, too. They also had to find a way to pay for the trip. The Merchant **Adventurers**, a group of London businessmen, offered to lend them money. To repay the loan, the Separatists would send furs, fish, and lumber back to London to sell. It took several months for them to agree on the terms of the loan. By that time it was June 1620, and the Separatists were still in Leiden, Holland. They had hoped to be in America by June to plant crops. Still, they were **determined** to go.

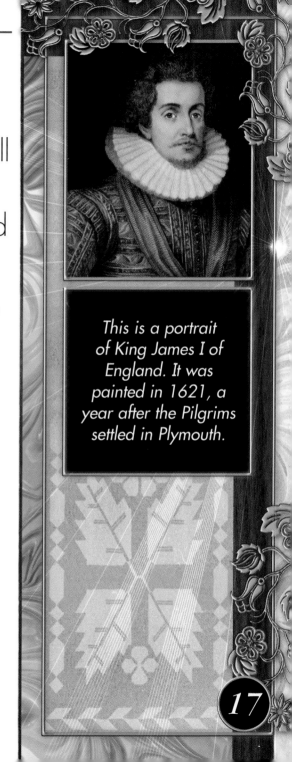

This is a portrait of King James I of England. It was painted in 1621, a year after the Pilgrims settled in Plymouth.

◀ This is a hand-colored woodcut of the Jamestown, Virginia Colony, in 1622.

17

Families were left behind as the Mayflower sailed away into the mist.

Leaving Leiden

Some of the Separatists sold their houses in Leiden and bought the *Speedwell,* a ship that would take them to America. Only 50 Separatists would go on this first trip to America. They would build some houses and would plant crops. Then the rest would follow. On about July 22, 1620, they said good-bye to Leiden and their friends and families. They had planned to sail to England first before going on to America. As they left Leiden, William Bradford wrote, "They left that goodly and pleasant city and knew they were pilgrims." It was the first time that anyone had called them Pilgrims.

This painting shows the Pilgrims leaving Holland to begin their journey to America. ▶

The Strangers

In England, the Merchant Adventurers said the Separatists had to take 67 other people with them. These people were farmers and **tradesmen** whose skills would be useful in a new colony. The Separatists called these people the Strangers. The Merchant Adventurers had rented the *Mayflower* to sail the Strangers to America. The Separatists would travel on the *Speedwell*. The *Speedwell* was a leaky boat. It was unsafe to sail and had to be left in England. Almost everyone moved onto the *Mayflower*. The *Mayflower* set sail for America on September 6, 1620.

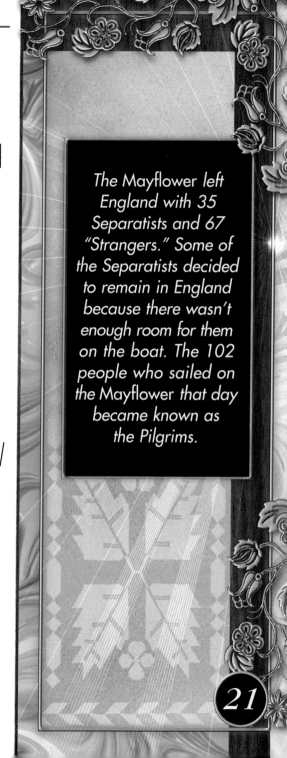

The *Mayflower* left England with 35 Separatists and 67 "Strangers." Some of the Separatists decided to remain in England because there wasn't enough room for them on the boat. The 102 people who sailed on the *Mayflower* that day became known as the Pilgrims.

◀ *This is a reconstruction of the Mayflower, the ship that carried the Pilgrims to America.*

21

When the first boatload of Pilgrims landed on the New England coast, John Alden and Mary Chilton were the first to set foot on American soil.

They Never Gave Up

Nothing came easy for the Separatists who became the Pilgrims. They had suffered religious persecution in England. They had given up their homes and even their families. Again and again, they had lost everything they owned. Many even gave up their lives for freedom of religion. Why didn't they give up? Being able to worship freely was more important to the Separatists than anything else. Their faith took them from England to Holland, and then to America. It guided the Pilgrims through many **hardships**. Their faith also became the **foundation** of a new nation, which became the United States.

Glossary

adventurers (ad-VEN-cher-erz) People who are willing to take risks.

Catholic (KATH-lik) Someone who belongs to the Roman Catholic religion.

Christians (KRIS-chunz) People who follow the teachings of Jesus Christ and the Bible.

climate (KLY-mit) The kind of weather a certain area has.

colony (KAH-luh-nee) An area in a new country that is still ruled by the leaders and laws of the old country.

determined (dih-TER-mihnd) To be very focused on doing something.

foundation (fown-DAY-shun) The part or basis upon which other parts are built.

hardships (HARD-ships) Things that cause people to suffer.

inherited (in-HEHR-it-ed) To have received the money or property of a person who has died.

merchants (MUR-chints) People who sell things.

persecution (pur-sih-KYOO-shun) Repeated cruel treatment of others, often because of their religious beliefs.

Separatists (SEH-puh-ruh-tists) People who belonged to a religious group that wanted to break away from the Church of England.

timber (TIM-bur) Wood that is cut and used for building houses, ships, and other wooden objects.

tradesmen (TRAYDZ-min) People who are trained to do special work with their hands.

weavers (WEE-vurz) People who weave thread into cloth.

Index

Web Sites

Due to the changing nature of Internet links, PowerKids Press has developed an online list of Web sites related to the subject of this book. This site is updated regularly. Please use this link to access the list:

www.powerkidslinks.com/lipil/pibmay/